T0132423

The Belling

by

John R. Durham

Adapted from a story told by his Grandmother

Illustrated

by

Hen Bo

AuthorHouse™ UK
1663 Liberty Drive
Bloomington, IN 47403 USA
www.authorhouse.co.uk
Phone: 0800.197.4150

Published by AuthorHouse 02/14/2017

ISBN: 978-1-5246-7753-4 (sc)
ISBN: 978-1-5246-7754-1 (e)

Print information available on the last page.

Any people depicted in stock imagery provided by Thinkstock are models,
and such images are being used for illustrative purposes only.
Certain stock imagery © Thinkstock.

This book is printed on acid-free paper.

authorHOUSE®

The Belling

by

John R. Durham

(Adapted from a story told by his Grandmother)

Bong, bong, bong... The church bells were ringing. Why? Wasn't it Saturday morning, my only morning of the week to sleep late? The bells weren't ringing their normal slow, methodical Sunday morning ring. They were ringing fast and furiously. I rolled out of bed, pulled back the curtains, and peered through the window at the street below. Everyone was rushing to the square. But why, was there some emergency in town.

Then my mother yelled from the kitchen downstairs, "Get up Johnny, it's a belling. Let's go, let's go!"

"A belling, what's a belling?" I shouted back as I pulled on my overalls and red flannel shirt that I had left on the chair from the night before. I knew it was something exciting as I looked back out the window while I tied up my boots. Everyone in our neighborhood was heading to the square, kids on bikes and homemade scooters, old couples walking arm in arm, teenagers and young couples hurrying down the middle of the street. Even farmer Brown was on his way mounted bareback on an old plow horse with two of his kids.

"Ma, what's a belling?" I yelled as I shot down the back stairs and into the kitchen. Where's everyone going? Why are the bells ringing? What happened? What's going on?"

Ma was busy running around the kitchen. She was gathering fruit, cookies and jam, and making sandwiches all at the same time. She answered, "Winnie and Lloyd got married. They're back from Bay Village. Everyone is going to the square for the belling. Hurry up, we have to go!"

Ma had a sense of excitement in her voice and her actions made me excited too! "But Ma, what's a belling?" I screamed out.

She answered, "It's a tradition here in Sunbury. It's tradition. Your Pa and I did it. Granny and Grandpa did it; everyone does it. It's great!" Then she handed me a brown paper bag full of rice and pulled on her sweater and pinned on her new hat. "Let's go, we can't be late." We rushed out the backdoor and down the drive, where we joined a long parade of people rushing to the square. Most of the people I knew. However, there were several unfamiliar faces. I didn't know everyone in town yet. And the neighborhood dogs were running around barking with excitement, like they understood what was going on.

Ma joined in with some ladies she knew and began talking. Franky, a kid from up the street, who was in my class, called out, "Hey Johnny, wait for me." I did. Franky was short for his age, but he sure was fast and strong and a good fighter. He almost always had a black eye. Franky and I had been best buddies since we had moved into town last year. We did everything together. We were in the same class at school and went to church together. The two of us spent most of our free time fishing and hiking and playing war in the woods around Alligator Pond. There wasn't really an alligator in the pond, but there was an old log that floated around sometimes that looked a little like one.

Franky knew all about the belling. He told me that when a man and woman get married, the man pushes his bride around the square in a wheelbarrow, while everyone throws rice. I was born and raised in Sunbury, but had only recently moved into town from a farm in the country. I was learning a lot by living in town and being closer to the action. My father had bought old man Nelson's house after he died. It was only five houses away from the square. The square was just down the hill.

We still had the farm; the Johnson family moved into our farmhouse after we moved to town. Mr. Johnson and his boys take care of the animals and help Pa with the fields. We grow corn, soy beans, and wheat. We have 23 cows, 3 horses, a billy-goat, and lots of chickens.

Pa had a new job now. He was the new butcher in Sam's Produce Market, the only store in town. Pa loved his new job and the extra money. Pa also liked being part of the social circle of town on a daily basis. There were always lots of people in the market, and everyone talked to him about their meat and chicken orders and their families and their problems. He knew everyone and everything.

Living in town meant that we were closer to the church, closer to school, and closer to our friends and family. Living in town was good. The best part was not having to get up at the crack of dawn to milk the cows before going to school. I didn't miss the cows.

So – this was my first belling. This is what living in town was all about. Excitement! Everyone was standing around the fountain, talking, anxiously awaiting Lloyd and Winnie's arrival. "Where were they? When would they show up?" I asked Franky.

"Don't worry, they will be here soon. Relax!"

"I can't. This is my first belling! What do I do? Where do we go?"

"Relax, just do what I do. Just watch and listen. Hey, there are some others guys from school and Miss Ross our teacher."

Winnie was the youngest of the Granger girls: Margarite, Elenore, Genevie, and Winagene, who everyone knew as Winnie. Her sisters were all older than she was. The Lord had blessed her mother and father with another baby girl after the other girls had grown, married, and moved out. The Granger girls had been known around town as the prettiest girls, and all the boys wanted to get to know them. They were polite, well mannered, and great cooks. Their family was the most talked about family in town.

Lloyd was the red-headed, freckled, friendly man who worked at the Sunbury News. He was born and raised on a farm just outside town. His brother and sister had bright red hair and lots of freckles as well. Lloyd was smart, he could read and write well and do math, but he was really known for his spelling and grammar. Lloyd could spell anything, and that came in very handy for his job as type-setter at the News. You rarely ever saw a missed spelled word in the News.

After dozens of people found their way to the square, Alton Wigton, Llyod's best friend, a tall, lanky young man, climbed up onto the fountain and introduced the newly married couple. "Ladies and gentlemen, may I have your attention please. We are gathered here today to celebrate and officially recognize the marriage of Lloyd and Winnie. As everyone knows, Lloyd is a hard-working, honest man. He graduated from Sunbury High School in 1933, one of the best in his class. He also has more freckles than anyone I know. And Winnie, well what can I say? She is a Granger Girl." Everyone in the square laughed. I really didn't know what was so funny. Alton continued, "The prettiest girls in north central Ohio. I'm still not sure how I let this one get away, and how Lloyd caught her. So, let's hear it for the new couple. Congratulations Lloyd, congratulations Winnie!"

The newly married couple joined Alton near the fountain, and a group of Winnie's girlfriends wheeled the noisiest wheelbarrow in the world up next to the couple. Winnie was nervously helped in, while Lloyd held it steady. As soon as she was seated, Lloyd yelled, "Hold on, Winnie, here we go!" He took off on a run as everyone started yelling, while running to line the sidewalk around the square, and throwing rice and birdseed. Little kids were chasing the couple screaming, and dogs followed them barking as they ran. Everyone was excited; this is what living in town was all about!

The wheelbarrow was painted with flowers and a big "Just Married" sign. A dozen tin cans were tied to the side and trailed behind, making it noisy. The tradition was to circle the square one time. By now, dozens of people, almost the whole town, were there. Lloyd was running fast and yelling to Winnie to hold on. You could tell Winnie wasn't having any fun. The metal wheel bounced up and down violently as it hit each brick paving the sidewalk.

As they passed me, I threw the rice that I had stuffed in my pockets. Most of it missed the target, but I didn't care. Franky was throwing the rice that he had as well. We loved every minute of this Sunbury, Ohio tradition.

After circling the square for the second time, Lloyd helped Winnie out of the wheelbarrow. She cursed, and everybody laughed. Granger girls never cursed. All the men shook Lloyd's hand and gave him big bear hugs. The ladies all kissed Winnie. It seemed as if they were all crying.

When the hugs and kisses were over, Lloyd jumped up onto the fountain and announced, "Everyone is welcome back to our house for cider, sandwiches, and cigars." Most of the group headed up the street to the couple's new house. Lloyd walked with his buddies, while Winnie walked with her girlfriends.

The excitement continued at the house. The men were outside on the porch and under the big oak tree in the front yard smoking cigars. All the ladies were in the kitchen getting the food ready to be served. Everyone was talking and laughing and having a great time. The little kids seemed to have climbed every tree in the neighborhood to get a good view of the activities.

The excitement continued to grow when a shiny new blue car pulled up in front of the house. Everyone stopped talking and turned to see who had arrived. It was Eleanor, Winnie's sister. She had just arrived from Columbus the State Capitol. She was dressed in a fancy city dress and was wearing white gloves and a mink. Her hat was small and had a blue little feather sticking out of the top. Eleanor was a fancy, high class lady. She had beautiful clothes, the nicest car, and a beautiful house in the city. A man opened the car door for her before she stepped out. He then reached into the backseat and handed her two large beautiful boxes with large bows. "Those are the biggest presents that I have ever seen. What could be in those boxes?" Franky whispered from the limb where we were sitting.

Hugs and kisses and introductions followed after Winnie and Eleanor finished their long greeting and walked into the house. "Why were they crying?" Franky wanted to know. "This was a happy day."

"Those are not sad tears, those are happy tears," I told Franky.

"Happy tears, what? I never saw anybody cry happy tears before. What are you talking about?"

17

"Trust me, those are tears of joy," I could see that Franky wasn't sure.

"Really?"

"Trust me. Happy tears."

Eventually the food was ready and everyone was called into the parlor for the blessing. "Dear Lord, bless this couple that we are celebrating with today. Bless their marriage, their families, and bless this food. Amen." The Reverend Barard must have been hungry, because that was the shortest prayer that I had ever heard him say. The reverend was a short muscular man. He was also known for being one of the strongest men in town. He was a high school football star and played at Otterbein College before becoming a minister. He had a booming voice, and no one could fall asleep in the First Methodist Church on Sunday morning when he was giving the message. We were now up on the front porch listening through the open window.

Everyone was served and sat down to eat. The conversations got quieter and the action calmed down. It wasn't as exciting as it had been earlier, so most of the kids, including Franky and me found other things to do. It was a Saturday morning after all, which meant no school; we couldn't waste the day around here. "Hey Franky, do you want to go fishing? I dug up some great big night crawlers last night after it rained."

"Sure! I'll run home get my stuff and meet you over at Alligator Pond.

"Hey, be careful and don't let that gator get you before I get there!"

"Don't worry, he won't get me. See ya in a little while."

The End

John Durham grew up in Columbus, Ohio and attended Otterbein College. After graduation, John started his overseas teaching career in Honduras, where he met his wife. His chosen career has taken him to countries in Latin America, the Caribbean, Central Asia, and China. John was a graduate teaching assistant at The University of Alabama while in graduate school. Roll Tide Roll!

John worked at The Capitol School in Tuscaloosa, Alabama for nine years. This non-traditional school is a multiple intelligence school, that is a showcase school for local universities and school systems. While working there, John took his students on camping trips and bike tours, and used Greenwood Cemetery to help teach about Alabama's history. His students wrote books too. The first student work was titled, The Jack Winn Story. Another student publication was titled, The Adventures of Rocket the Turtle.

John started working for Quality Schools International (QSI) in 2004. This organization has 37 schools in 30 countries. The QSI philosophy is very similar to William Glasser's mastery learning approach.

John encourages teachers and parents to help instill a love of reading and writing in their children.
Mr. Durham's philosophy is that education must be meaningful and memorable.

Printed in the United States
By Bookmasters